ALBANIA: HUMAN RIGHTS

EXECUTIVE SUMMARY

The Republic of Albania is a parliamentary democracy. The constitution vests legislative authority in the unicameral parliament (Assembly), which elects both the prime minister and the president. The prime minister heads the government, while the president has limited executive power. On June 23, the country held parliamentary elections, which the Organization for Security and Cooperation in Europe (OSCE) Office for Democratic Institutions and Human Rights (ODIHR) reported were competitive and respected fundamental freedoms but were conducted in an atmosphere of distrust that tainted the electoral environment. Security forces reported to civilian authorities. Security forces committed human rights abuses.

The most significant human rights problems were: pervasive corruption in all branches of government, and particularly within the judicial system; the stalling of the reform agenda, in particular the fight against corruption, as the political parties focused on the June elections; and domestic violence and discrimination against women.

Other human rights problems included police beating and other mistreatment of suspects during detention and interrogation, sometimes to elicit confessions; substandard prison conditions; an inefficient judiciary subject to political pressure and corruption; and child abuse. Displaced and street children remained a problem, particularly within the Romani community. Marginalization and abuse of the Romani and Balkan Egyptian communities were serious problems. Discrimination on the basis of sexual orientation and gender identity was a problem. Cases of trafficking in persons continued to be reported.

Impunity remained a problem. Government efforts to prosecute officials who committed abuses were sporadic and inconsistent. Government officials and politicians, as well as judges and those with powerful business interests, often were able to avoid prosecution. Some lower-level officials were punished for abuses. Some government officials, who were clearly implicated in abuse cases, were removed and given other government positions without any penalty.

Section 1. Respect for the Integrity of the Person, Including Freedom from:

a. Arbitrary or Unlawful Deprivation of Life

In September an appeals court considering the 2011 killing of four protesters in front of the prime minister's office sustained the acquittal of Republican Guard Margarit Kume for obstruction of justice, but it found Republican Guards Ndrea Prendi and Agim Llupo guilty of the lesser charge of negligent homicide and sentenced them to one and three years in prison, respectively. Time served counted against their sentences. In October prosecutors appealed the case to the Supreme Court, seeking sentences of 23 and 25 years for Prendi and Llupo, respectively.

During the year the government cooperated with the European Union Special Investigative Task Force investigation into allegations that the Kosovo Liberation Army and affiliates detained civilian "prisoners of war" from Kosovo at locations in Albania, held them under inhuman conditions, killed them between 1999 and mid-2000, and then trafficked their organs.

Incidents of societal killings, including both "blood feud" and revenge killings, occurred during the year. Such killings sometimes involved criminal gangs. Although long-standing traditions surrounding blood feuds prohibit killing children or women, nongovernmental organizations (NGOs) reported cases in which perpetrators intentionally targeted minors or women. The ombudsman reported cases in which authorities refused to protect families or prevent blood feud killings.

The Children's Rights Center of Albania reported three blood feud killings during the year. Other NGOs reported higher numbers of blood feud killings, but data were unreliable. Blood feud cases are tried by district courts. The law punishes premeditated murder, when committed for revenge or a blood feud, with 20 years' or life imprisonment.

b. Disappearance

There were no reports of politically motivated disappearances.

c. Torture and Other Cruel, Inhuman, or Degrading Treatment or Punishment

While the constitution and law prohibit such actions, police and prison guards sometimes beat and abused suspects and detainees.

The ombudsman is mandated by law through the National Mechanism for the Prevention of Torture (NMPT) to monitor and report on prisons and detention centers. During the year the ombudsman and NGOs reported that conditions in most prisons and detention centers improved, although serious problems remained in some facilities. In 2012 the ombudsman received 386 complaints from prisoners and detainees claiming physical abuse or torture, unlawful detention, illegal search and seizures, unlawful fines, violation of privacy, humiliation, and failure to properly provide information. The ombudsman also reported a lack of proper medical attention in many facilities, as well as poor living conditions.

The Albanian Helsinki Committee (AHC) reported that police sometimes used excessive force or that the conditions of certain facilities in which police kept detainees were of such poor standards as to constitute inhuman treatment. The majority of the complaints involved unjustified stops by police, detention past legal deadlines, failure to make citizens aware of their rights when detained, and poor conditions of detention centers. The AHC stated that police often reported that detainees claiming abuse arrived with preexisting injuries.

NGOs reported that complaints from juvenile detainees about physical abuse or violence within detention centers and prisons were rarely taken seriously.

During the year the ombudsman reported that the prosecutor initially accepted his 2012 request to open a criminal investigation into the allegation that five guards tortured two prisoners in Tirana's Jordan Misja prison but later dropped the case.

Prison and Detention Center Conditions

Prison and detention center conditions varied significantly by facility. The country was in the process of replacing some older facilities where conditions were harsh and life threatening, while newer facilities built after 1991 generally met international standards. Conditions under the control of the Ministry of Justice were generally better than those under the control of the Ministry of Interior.

Physical Conditions: As of October there were 2,090 persons in pretrial detention centers and 3,111 convicted persons in prisons, including 87 female prisoners and 104 juveniles. Authorities held men and women in separate facilities, with pretrial detainees held separately from convicted prisoners. Conditions of the female prison and of female detention centers were generally better than those of male facilities.

As of October there were nine deaths in prisons: seven due to natural causes, one suicide, and one death that authorities were investigating, according to the ombudsman. During the year the prosecutor declined to investigate the 2012 case of the death of a prisoner who allegedly had been denied medical attention and restrained in his bed, and who was found covered in urine and fecal matter after he had died in his cell.

Older facilities had inadequate access to potable water, sanitation, ventilation, lighting, and health care. Older facilities had unhygienic conditions and lacked many basic amenities. In addition mistreatment by guards and other prisoners threatened the lives and health of prisoners and detainees. The ombudsman and the AHC reported that detainees and prisoners did not have adequate access to medical examinations and other services.

The Ministry of the Interior maintained police stations and temporary detention facilities. Conditions in those facilities were completely inadequate. In some cases they were unheated during the winter. Some lacked basic hygienic amenities such as showers or sinks, had limited access to toilets and little or no ventilation or access to natural light, lacked beds or benches, and had cramped conditions.

Administration: NGOs noted that in many institutions recordkeeping was not adequate. Prisoners and detainees have the right to meet relatives, and meetings can occur up to four times per month for adults and up to eight times for juveniles. Prisoners and detainees were free to exercise their religion, and some facilities had special places for religious services. Prisoners and detainees were permitted to submit complaints to the ombudsman and to judicial and administrative authorities. Every penal installation had a mailbox in which prisoners and detainees were entitled to submit complaints without censorship. Prisoners could meet confidentially with the ombudsman, the Prisons Supervisory Commission, or foreign and domestic human rights NGOs. The ombudsman reported that prison officials generally cooperated with their investigations; however, prisons did not fully implement the ombudsman's recommendations. NGOs reported that the government took their suggestions more seriously but continued to refuse to investigate some cases. The country used alternatives to incarceration in sentencing.

Authorities investigated credible allegations of inhuman conditions and documented the results of their investigations. The ombudsman found corruption to be a serious problem in detention centers, particularly with special release programs. There were several reports that prisoners received permission to participate in special release programs after bribing prison officials.

Independent Monitoring: The government allowed local and international human rights groups, the media, and the International Committee of the Red Cross, as well as international bodies such as the Committee for the Prevention of Torture, to monitor prison conditions.

Improvements: The ombudsman and NGOs reported that conditions in most prisons and detention centers improved during the year. The NMPT increased its number of inspections by 41 percent yet received 48 percent fewer complaints against the police and prisons. During the year the government finished construction on three new predetention facilities and began construction on two others. Two older facilities were closed by year's end. The director general of the prisons system ordered all prisons and detention systems to improve recordkeeping, in line with the ombudsman's recommendations. Recordkeeping improved through an electronic system.

d. Arbitrary Arrest or Detention

The law and constitution prohibit arbitrary arrest and detention; however, there were reports that the police occasionally arbitrarily arrested and detained persons.

Role of the Police and Security Apparatus

The Ministry of Interior oversees the police. The state police are the main organization responsible for internal security. The Republican Guard protects high-level state officials, foreign dignitaries, and certain state properties. The Ministry of Defense oversees the country's armed forces, which also assist the population in times of humanitarian need. The State Intelligence Service (SHISH) gathers information and carries out foreign intelligence and counterintelligence activities.

Civilian authorities generally maintained effective control over the state police, Republican Guard, armed forces, and SHISH, although periodically state resources were used for personal gain and members of the security forces committed abuses.

State police officers did not always enforce the law equally. Personal associations, political or criminal connections, poor infrastructure, and lack of equipment or inadequate supervision often influenced enforcement of laws. Low salaries, poor motivation and leadership, and a lack of diversity in the workforce contributed to continued corruption and unprofessional behavior. Impunity remained a serious problem, and few police officers were prosecuted for abuses.

The government has mechanisms to investigate and punish abuse and corruption. The government's Internal Control Service conducted audits, responded to complaints, and carried out investigations with increased emphasis on human rights, prison conditions, and adherence to standard operating procedures; however, there were widespread reports that police sometimes accepted bribes in return for not issuing citations or not entering personal information into crime databases.

During the year the ombudsman processed complaints against police officers mainly on arrest and detention problems. The ombudsman received 139 complaints as of October and investigated or provided counsel in 107 cases.

The European Commission reported that during the year the police signed a cooperation agreement with a third NGO to monitor detention facilities, including unannounced visits. The commission reported that all police officers were trained in human rights, and the Istanbul Protocol on documentation of mistreatment was expanded from prisons to district police commissariats. The prisons directorate approved guidelines on hunger strike management. The ombudsman, through the NMPT, reported greater cooperation by security forces with investigations and increased implementation of his recommendations on mistreatment.

Arrest Procedures and Treatment of Detainees

The constitution requires that a judge issue a warrant for a suspect's arrest based on sufficient evidence. There were no reports of secret arrests. Under the law police must immediately inform the prosecutor of an arrest. The prosecutor may release the suspect or petition the court within 48 hours to hold the individual further. A court must decide within 48 hours whether to place a suspect in detention, require bail, prohibit travel, or require the defendant to report regularly to the police. Prosecutors requested and courts routinely ordered detention in many criminal cases. Nevertheless, courts routinely denied prosecutors' requests for detention of well-connected, high-profile defendants.

The constitution requires that authorities inform detained persons immediately of the charges against them and of their rights; however, this right was not always respected. There is not an effective system for handling the monetary aspect of bail. Instead, courts often order suspects to report to police or prosecutors on a weekly basis. Authorities allowed detainees prompt access to an attorney, at public expense if necessary. Many suspects were ordered to remain under house arrest, often at their own request, because they received credit for serving this time if they were convicted. House arrest was not monitored effectively, and suspects could move outside freely without being detected by authorities.

Under the law detained persons should be transferred to the custody of the Ministry of Justice, which has facilities more adequate for long-term inmates, if their custody will exceed 10 hours. Due to poor communication between the ministries, this seldom happened, and it was common for persons, including juveniles, to remain in police detention centers for long periods.

Arbitrary Arrest: Police occasionally detained persons for inordinate amounts of time for questioning without formally arresting them.

Pretrial Detention: While the law requires completion of most pretrial investigations within three months, a prosecutor may extend this period to two years or longer. The law provides that the maximum pretrial detention should not exceed three years; there were no reports that authorities violated this limit during the year. Lengthy pretrial detentions often occurred due to delayed investigations, defense mistakes, or the intentional failure of defense counsel to appear. Under the law a judge cannot hold an attorney in contempt of court for failure to appear to prevent such delaying actions by attorneys. Limited material resources, lack of space, poor court calendar management, insufficient staff, and failure of attorneys and witnesses to appear prevented the court system from adjudicating cases in a timely fashion. As of October, 40 percent of the prison/detainee population was in pretrial detention.

e. Denial of Fair Public Trial

The constitution provides for an independent judiciary; however, political pressure, intimidation, widespread corruption, and limited resources sometimes prevented the judiciary from functioning independently and efficiently. Additionally, court hearings were often closed to the public. Court security officers routinely refused entry to hearings and routinely called the presiding judge in each case to ask if the person seeking admission could attend the hearing. Some agencies routinely disregarded court orders. The politicization of appointments to the High Court and Constitutional Court threatened to undermine the independence and integrity of these institutions.

Trial Procedures

The law provides that defendants are presumed innocent until convicted. The law provides for defendants to be informed promptly and in detail of the charges, with free interpretation as necessary, and to a fair and public trial without undue delay. The court system does not provide for jury trials. Defendants have the right to consult with an attorney, and to have one provided at public expense if they cannot afford one. The law provides defendants with adequate time and facilities to prepare defense, and to access government-held evidence. Defendants have the right to confront witnesses against them and present witness and evidence in their defense. Defendants may not to be compelled to testify or confess guilt. Defendants have the right to appeal. The government generally respected these rights.

Political Prisoners and Detainees

There were no reports of political prisoners or detainees. Former political prisoners under the communist regime continued to petition the government for compensation. On several occasions throughout the year, groups of former political prisoners attempted to protest the government's failure to pay them legally mandated compensation. In nearly every case, authorities prevented the protest from occurring and arrested organizers.

Civil Judicial Procedures and Remedies

While individuals and organizations may seek civil remedies for human rights violations, courts were susceptible to corruption, inefficiency, intimidation, and political tampering. Many court hearings were held in judges' offices, which contributed to a lack of professionalism and opportunities for corruption. These factors undermined the judiciary's authority, contributed to controversial court decisions, and led to an inconsistent application of civil law.

Regional Human Rights Court Decisions

Citizens could appeal decisions involving alleged violations of the European Convention on Human Rights by the state to the European Court of Human Rights. The court issued 30 judgments against the country, of which three were not fully executed.

Property Restitution

A large number of conflicting claims for private and religious property confiscated during the communist era remained unresolved. World Bank experts asserted that given the slow pace of restitution, the government would need $38.6 billion and 30 years to complete the process. The government did not implement an effective system for restoring properties confiscated during the communist era.

On April 23, a private bailiff's office evicted at gunpoint 14 families from an apartment complex in Tirana, allegedly enforcing a court order returning the property to its procommunist-era owner. The families launched a hunger strike to demand the government provide them with recourse. The Tirana prosecutor's office initiated criminal proceedings against city government agencies that initially issued the court order, and the evicted families initiated civil proceedings against the private bailiff's office. As of October the cases continued.

f. Arbitrary Interference with Privacy, Family, Home, or Correspondence

Incidents where the government seized or attempted to seize property without due process occurred during the year. In November the National Urban Construction Inspectorate (INUK) supported by state police attempted to evict owners from their homes in an apartment building in Vlore. These families held property titles from the respective property registry office. They reported being prevented from entering their homes by police while being told that the government was sequestering the building for demolition. The ombudsman reported that the actions of the government violated due process. Government officials claimed that the building was illegally built and violated the conditions of its permit. The regional Administrative Court of Vlore ruled in favor of the building's residents and ordered the government to suspend its actions.

Section 2. Respect for Civil Liberties, Including:

a. Freedom of Speech and Press

The constitution provides for freedom of speech and press, and the government generally respected these rights. There were reports that the government and businesses influenced and pressured the media.

Freedom of Speech: Individuals could generally criticize the government publicly or privately without reprisal; however, there were reports that the government required employees to attend campaign rallies.

Members of a group of former political prisoners from the communist regime who petitioned for government compensation reported that state security officials constantly monitored their movements and harassed them and their family members.

Freedom of Press: The independent media were active and largely unrestrained, although there were cases of direct and indirect political and economic pressure on the media, including threats against journalists. At times political pressure and lack of funding constrained the independent print media, and journalists reported that they practiced self-censorship. Political parties, trade unions, and other groups published newspapers or magazines independent of government influence.

In its annual Media Sustainability Index, the nongovernmental organization IREX noted that the independence of the media in the country neither improved nor deteriorated compared with the previous year.

The government controlled the editorial line of the public Albanian Radio and Television, which operated a national television channel and a national radio station and, by law, received 50 percent of its budget from the government. While private stations generally operated free of direct government influence, most owners believed that the content of their broadcasts could influence government action toward their other businesses. Business owners also freely used media outlets to gain favor and promote their interests with both major parties. Many media owners courted government leaders to gain favors or avoid taxes.

The media reported that the government distributed public funds for advertisements to media outlets based on personal and political favoritism rather than viewership or readership.

Violence and Harassment: There were incidents of violence against members of the broadcast media during the year, and political and business actors subjected journalists to pressure.

On April 7, police detained Gent Ballta, a cameraman of national commercial television station Top Channel, after a soccer match that led to confrontations between soccer club fans and police officers. Ballta said that he was filming the confrontations and that police detained him along with fans. While in detention in Tirana's police station, he alleged that police assaulted him before he was later freed. Police first denied the assault and in a statement a day later claimed they detained Ballta briefly because he refused to identify himself. The state police later suspended the official who allegedly committed the assault and opened a disciplinary investigation against him.

Censorship or Content Restrictions: Journalists complained that publishers and editors censored their work directly and indirectly in response to political and commercial pressures. Many journalists complained that a lack of employment contracts frequently hindered their ability to report objectively and encouraged them to practice self-censorship.

The Union of Albanian Journalists stated in September that in 75 percent of the country's media outlets, there were delays of two to four months in the payment of reporters' monthly salaries. These delays led some journalists to more heavily rely on outside sources of income, which biased their reporting.

Broadcasters and publishers complained that the government used its purchases of advertising to leverage favorable reporting from media outlets. Private advertisers tended to do the same due to fear of tax inspections.

Libel Laws/National Security: The law grants special protection to national and foreign government officials in defamation cases; however, the law prohibits insult and deliberate publication of defamatory information as privately prosecuted misdemeanors subject to a fine.

Some media outlets continued to produce investigative stories, which sometimes led to dismissals and criminal cases against corrupt public officials.

In 2012 the Tirana District Court fined Top Channel 51 million leks ($489,300) for the 2009 broadcast of hidden camera footage that led to the dismissal of former minister of culture, youth, and sports Ylli Pango. The court of appeals overturned the decision. The High Court ruled that the case be sent back to the district court. Pango's lawyers appealed the ruling, and the High Court had not heard the case as of October.

Internet Freedom

There were no government restrictions on access to the internet or reports that the government monitored e-mail or internet chat rooms without appropriate legal authority. According to data compiled by the International Telecommunication Union, approximately 55 percent of the population used the internet in 2012. The number of individuals who subscribed to mobile broadband internet in 2012 reached 18 percent, while the number of individuals that subscribed to fixed broadband internet in 2012 was 5 percent. Fixed broadband was concentrated mostly in urban areas.

Academic Freedom and Cultural Events

There were no government restrictions on academic freedom or cultural events; however, corruption in educational institutions, including public universities, was widespread and often affected student performance. Many students complained that teachers demanded bribes to pass courses, making it difficult for some students to obtain higher education.

b. Freedom of Peaceful Assembly and Association

Freedom of Assembly

The constitution and law provide for freedom of assembly, and the government generally respected it.

Prior to the June 23 elections, some party supporters reported that police harassed participants or prevented them from holding public rallies. ODHIR reported that fundamental freedoms were respected and that all contestants were able to campaign freely.

Freedom of Association

The constitution and law provide for freedom of association, and the government generally respected it.

c. Freedom of Religion

See the Department of State's *International Religious Freedom Report* at www.state.gov/j/drl/irf/rpt/.

d. Freedom of Movement, Internally Displaced Persons, Protection of Refugees, and Stateless Persons

The constitution and law provide for freedom of internal movement, foreign travel, emigration, and repatriation, and the government generally respected these rights. The government cooperated with the Office of the UN High Commissioner for Refugees (UNHCR) and other humanitarian organizations in providing protection and assistance to refugees, returning refugees, asylum seekers, stateless persons, and other persons of concern.

In-country Movement: Internal migrants must transfer their civil registration to their new community of residence to receive government services and must prove they are legally domiciled through property ownership, a property rental agreement, or utility bills. Many persons could not provide this proof and thus lacked access to essential services. Other citizens lacked formal registration in the communities in which they resided, particularly Roma and Balkan-Egyptians. The law does not prohibit their registration, but it was often difficult to complete.

Protection of Refugees

Access to Asylum: The law provides for the granting of asylum or refugee status, and the government has established a system for providing protection to refugees. There is no time limit for requesting asylum, but the law provides that the government must make a decision regarding the granting of asylum within 101 days of the initial request. The government generally complied with this requirement.

Safe Country of Origin/Transit: The law prohibits individuals from safe countries of origin to apply for asylum or refugee status. There were no credible complaints that asylum seekers were sent to countries with poorly functioning asylum systems.

Durable Solutions: In May the government agreed to accept 210 Mujahedin-e Khalq individuals from Iraq, whom the government classified as asylum seekers. It resettled 196 of them near Tirana as of October. The government assisted the safe, voluntary return of one refugee from Egypt and one from Tunisia.

Temporary Protection: The government also provided temporary protection to individuals who may not qualify as refugees. The government reported there were no refugees seeking temporary protection during the year.

Stateless Persons

In 2011 the UNHCR reported 7,443 stateless persons in the country.

Section 3. Respect for Political Rights: The Right of Citizens to Change Their Government

The constitution provides citizens the right to change their government peacefully, and citizens exercised this right through periodic elections based on universal suffrage.

Elections and Political Participation

Recent Elections: On June 23, the country held parliamentary elections that the OSCE/ODIHR election observation mission reported "were competitive with active citizen participation throughout the campaign and genuine respect for fundamental freedoms." The OSCE also noted, however, that "the atmosphere of distrust between the two main political forces tainted the electoral environment and challenged the administration of the entire electoral process." The observation mission also cited problems with procedural irregularities and instances of inappropriate overlap between state institutions and party interests.

The Central Election Commission (CEC) operated without a quorum throughout the elections due to a boycott by members of the opposition party following the controversial dismissal by the prime minister of one of its members. The OSCE reported that many persons were under the impression that the CEC acted politically, which contributed to an overall public sense of distrust.

Participation of Women and Minorities: The law mandates that women fill 30 percent of appointed and elected positions, and the electoral code provides that 30 percent of candidates should be women. Not all parties followed the electoral code, and fines for noncompliance were low. On May 11, the CEC fined the Democratic Party, Socialist Party, and Socialist Movement for Integration for failing to comply with legally mandated quotas in their candidate lists for the June parliamentary elections. There were 25 women elected to the 140-seat assembly in the June 23 elections, an increase from 22 in the previous parliament. The number of female ministers in the new government increased to six, compared with one in the previous government.

Civil registration requirements and lack of identification among the Romani population made it difficult for many Roma to participate in the June 23 elections. Media published reports of attempts to confiscate voter identification from Romani voters in exchange for money or food prior to the elections. There were no Roma elected to the assembly or serving in ministerial or subministerial positions. Several members of the Greek minority who belonged to different political parties were elected to the assembly; a prominent individual from a party representing the Greek minority was elected deputy speaker of the parliament in September.

Section 4. Corruption and Lack of Transparency in Government

The law provides criminal penalties for corruption by officials; however, the government did not implement the law effectively, and officials frequently engaged in corrupt practices with impunity.

Corruption: Corruption in all branches of government was pervasive. From January through June, Joint Investigative Units (JIUs), multiagency units that investigate and prosecute public corruption and other financial crimes, began 651 new investigations and sent 230 cases to court. Trials concluded for 82 cases, rendering guilty verdicts for 122 defendants and dismissing cases against 19 defendants. As of June, 275 individuals were still in trial.

On October 24, a court sentenced former prosecutor Sander Plepi to one year in prison for unlawful influence on his wife Marsela Balili, a judge in the same district court, but acquitted the wife.

In 2012 overall coordination of anticorruption matters was assigned to the Department of Internal Auditing and Control (DIACA), in the Prime Minister's Office. DIACA conducted a number of its own investigations into corruption complaints but produced no significant reports and referred no cases for prosecution. It was generally considered ineffective.

The Albanian State Police Economic Crime and Corruption Section investigated corruption cases. The section's investigations were hampered by a limited capacity for undercover investigations and surveillance. Other agencies, including tax and customs authorities, and state auditors and regulators also perform anticorruption investigations. Their efforts, as well as the efforts of the state police, were hampered by investigative leaks, real and perceived political pressure, and a haphazard reassignment system.

Prosecutions were handled by the Office of the Prosecutor General through JIUs. There were seven units in the nation's largest cities. The units made significant progress in pursuing low-level public corruption, but prosecution of higher-level crimes remained elusive, due to investigators' fear of retribution, a general lack of resources, and judicial corruption.

Enforcement agencies did not actively and sustainably collaborate with civil society in most cases. Enforcement agencies were sufficiently resourced. Agencies cooperated in selective instances that international actors brought to their attention, in many instances at the request of civil society. The government's use of slogans promoting "zero tolerance" of corruption often suppressed reporting and promoted data manipulation indicating that corruption did not exist.

Authorities removed some government officials who were clearly implicated in abuse cases but gave them other government positions without any penalty. Prosecuting higher-level officials remained problematic, and high-profile defendants usually were found not guilty, even in the face of overwhelming evidence.

Whistleblower Protection: The law does not provide protection for whistleblowers.

Financial Disclosure: The law requires public officials to disclose their assets to the High Inspectorate for the Declaration and Audit of Assets (HIDAA), which monitored and verified such disclosures. HIDAA made these disclosures available to the public. The law provided for HIDAA to fine officials who failed to comply with disclosure requirements. As of October HIDAA fined 252 individuals for delaying their submissions and for conflict of interest.

In October HIDAA personnel pressed criminal charges against HIDAA's chief inspector Zana Xhuka, accusing Xhuka of stealing public funds, manipulating asset declarations, and misusing personnel. Xhuka claimed the charges were politically motivated.

Public Access to Information: The law provides for public access to government information, but the government did not effectively implement the law. The process for making the information public often was not clear, and officials were sometimes reluctant to release information. The law stipulates that the right to access information can be restricted when information is categorized as classified or when such a release would violate the protection of personal data. The law specifies a 40-day time frame for the responsible public institutions to provide the required information. Most government ministries and agencies posted public information directly on their websites; however, businesses and citizens complained of a lack of transparency and the failure to publish some regulations or legislation that should be basic public information. Citizens often faced serious problems in obtaining such information. Generally, accessing government information is free of charge, but there are specific cases in which processing fees are required to cover the cost of service for the institution providing the information. Noncompliance is punishable as an administrative rather than a criminal offense. Citizens may appeal denials of disclosure with the authority with which they filed the original request or in a civil court.

Section 5. Governmental Attitude Regarding International and Nongovernmental Investigation of Alleged Violations of Human Rights

A number of domestic and international human rights groups generally operated without government restriction, investigating and publishing their findings on human rights cases. Government officials generally cooperated and responded to their views.

Government Human Rights Bodies: The Office of the Ombudsman is the main human rights institution for promoting and enforcing human rights. The ombudsman has the authority to inspect detention and prison facilities and initiate some cases in which a victim is unable to come forward. Although the ombudsman lacked the power to enforce decisions, he acted as a monitor for human rights violations. The ombudsman reports to the assembly annually.

The assembly has a committee on legal issues, public administration, and human rights. This committee was ineffective, however, on human rights problems and as of September did not respond to requests to meet with the ombudsman.

Cases of discrimination may be brought to the government's anti-discrimination commissioner; however, the commissioner's office focused primarily on advocacy and awareness campaigns, levying very few sanctions against government officials. The law allows the antidiscrimination commissioner to testify as an expert witness, even in appeals on cases the office rejected. Two cases were presented in court testing enforcement of the law. The court ruled that discrimination took place in one case, which was under appeal at year's end, and as of October it did not issue a ruling on the second case.

Section 6. Discrimination, Societal Abuses, and Trafficking in Persons

The law prohibits discrimination on the basis of race, gender, age, disability, language, religion, gender identity and/or sexual orientation, health, family, economic, or social status; however, the government did not effectively enforce these prohibitions.

Women

Rape and Domestic Violence: The criminal code penalizes rape, including spousal rape, but the government did not enforce these laws effectively. Victims rarely reported spousal abuse, and officials did not prosecute spousal rape. The concept of spousal rape was not well established, and authorities and the public often did not consider it a crime. The law imposes penalties for rape and assault depending on the age of the victim. For rape of an adult, the prison term is three to 10 years; for rape of an adolescent between the ages of 14 and 18, the term is five to 15 years; and for rape of a child under 14, the term is seven to 15 years.

Domestic violence against women, including spousal abuse, remained a serious problem. As of October police reported 2,130 cases of domestic violence, compared with 1,860 cases during the same period in 2012. The government pressed charges in 825 cases, compared with 593 cases during the same period in 2012. The courts issued 1,306 restraining orders as of October, compared with 1,146 orders issued during the same period in 2012. Police reported they received 2,515 domestic violence-related complaints through their emergency hotline as of October, compared with 1,405 complaints received over the same period in 2012. Police often did not have the training or capacity to deal effectively with domestic violence cases.

The Ministry of Youth and Social Welfare oversees women's issues, including domestic violence. The government shelter for domestic violence victims in Tirana assisted 27 women and 27 children as of November; however, the shelter could not accept victims without a court order. NGOs operated three shelters to protect victims from domestic violence, one in Tirana and two outside the capital.

Sexual Harassment: The law prohibits sexual harassment; however, officials rarely enforced the law. NGOs believe that sexual harassment was severely underreported.

Reproductive Rights: Couples and individuals have the right to decide freely and responsibly the number, spacing, and timing of their children, and they have the information and means to do so free from discrimination, coercion, and violence. Under the law health care is provided to all citizens. The quality of and access to care, however, including obstetric and postpartum care, was not satisfactory, especially in the remote rural areas. According to the Demographic and Health Survey, only 11 percent of the population used modern contraceptive methods. To address these issues, the Ministry of Health launched a new family planning strategy with the assistance of the United Nations Population Fund (UNFPA) for the period 2012-16. The strategy sought to increase the demand for and access to quality reproductive health and family planning services through increasing the prevalence of contraceptive use, to reduce the number of unwanted pregnancies, and to improve maternal and child health.

Discrimination: The law provides equal rights for men and women under family law and property law and in the judicial system. Women were not excluded from any occupation in either law or practice, but they were underrepresented at the highest levels of their fields. Although the law mandates equal pay for equal work, the government and employers did not fully implement this provision. In many communities women were subjected to societal discrimination as a result of traditional social norms that considered women to be subordinate to men.

Gender-based Sex Selection: A December 2012 study by World Vision and UNFPA claimed that there may be gender-based sex selection occurring in the country, although accurate data were difficult to obtain.

Children

Birth Registration: Citizenship is derived by birth within the country's territory or from a parent. In general parents are encouraged to register the birth of a child in a timely manner. A monetary reward for registrations completed within 60 days of birth is provided to further incentivize early registration. There were no reports of discrimination in birth registration; however, residency requirements for registration made it more difficult for many Romani and Balkan-Egyptian parents to register their children and access some other government services that were dependent on registration.

According to the Children's Rights Center of Albania (CRCA), children born to internal migrants or those returning from abroad frequently had no birth certificates or other legal documentation and as a result were unable to attend school. This was particularly a problem for Romani families, in which couples often married young and failed to register the birth of their children.

Education: The law provides for nine years of free education and authorizes private schools. School attendance is mandatory through the ninth grade or until age 16, whichever occurs first. Many children left school earlier than the law allows to work with their families, particularly in rural areas. Parents must purchase supplies, books, uniforms, and space heaters for some classrooms, which were prohibitively expensive for many families, particularly Roma and other minorities. Many families also cited these costs as a reason for not sending girls to school. Although the government has a program to provide free textbooks for low-income families, many families and NGOs reported that they were unable to acquire the free textbooks.

Child Abuse: Child abuse, including sexual abuse, occurred, although victims rarely reported it. The CRCA reported that 58 percent of children were victims of physical abuse, 11 percent of children were victims of sexual harassment, and almost 5 percent of children reported that they had been victims of sexual abuse. Almost 70 percent of children reported psychological abuse from family members, according to the CRCA.

Forced and Early Marriage: The minimum age for marriage is 18. Underage marriages occurred mostly in rural areas and within Romani communities. According to 2009 UNFPA statistics, 9.6 percent of women between the ages of 20 and 24 were married before they were 18. The UNFPA reported that in 2011, 31 percent of the 13- to 17-year-old women from the Romani community were married. Some NGOs reported that early and forced marriages occurred in rural communities as part of human trafficking schemes, when parents consented for their underage girls to marry older foreign men, who subsequently trafficked them to other countries.

Sexual Exploitation of Children: In some cases children under the age of 18 were exploited in prostitution. The penalties for the commercial sexual exploitation of children range from fines to 15 years' imprisonment. The country has a statutory rape law, and the minimum age of consensual sex is 14. The penalty for statutory rape of a child under the age of 14 is a prison term of five to 15 years. The law prohibits making or distributing child pornography; penalties are a fine of one million to five million leks ($9,590 to $47,950) and a prison sentence of one to five years. In May, with the input of NGOs and the ombudsman, the parliament passed a law criminalizing the possession of child pornography. Laws concerning rape and sexual exploitation of minors were generally enforced effectively; however, NGOs reported that laws enforcing child pornography were rarely enforced.

Displaced Children: Displaced and street children remained a problem, particularly within the Romani community. Street children begged or did petty work; some migrated to neighboring countries, particularly during the summer. These children were at highest risk of trafficking, and some became trafficking victims. Some displaced children were used by criminal gangs to burglarize homes because the law prohibits prosecuting children under the age of 14 for burglary. Very few child trafficking cases were prosecuted.

Institutionalized Children: There were reports that orphans leaving the custody of the state at adulthood faced significant challenges finding adequate housing and services.

International Child Abductions: The country is a party to the 1980 Hague Convention on the Civil Aspects of International Child Abduction. For information see the Department of State's report on compliance at www.travel.state.gov/abduction/resources/congressreport/congressreport_4308.html.

Anti-Semitism

There were reportedly only a few hundred Jews living in the country. There were no reports of anti-Semitic acts.

Trafficking in Persons

See the Department of State's *Trafficking in Persons Report* at www.state.gov/j/tip/.

Persons with Disabilities

The constitution and laws prohibit discrimination against persons with physical, sensory, intellectual, and mental disabilities in employment, education, transportation, access to health care, and the provision of other state services. Despite these legal prohibitions, employers, schools, health-care providers, and providers of other state services sometimes discriminated against persons with disabilities. The law mandates that new public buildings be accessible to persons with disabilities, but the government only sporadically enforced the law.

According to the 2011 census, 24 percent of persons with disabilities had never attended school, and 65 percent of such persons were female. Widespread poverty, unregulated working conditions, and poor medical care posed significant problems for many persons with disabilities.

Persons with disabilities were not restricted from participating in civic affairs, although resource constraints and lack of infrastructure made it difficult for them to participate fully in many activities. The government set up social services agencies to protect the rights of persons with disabilities, but the agencies often lacked funding to implement their programs. The law does not limit the right of persons with disabilities to vote; however, voting centers were often were located in facilities lacking accommodations for such persons, effectively undermining their right to vote. During the June 23 elections, many voting centers were located in upper levels of schools and public buildings without any access for voters with disabilities.

The ombudsman regularly inspected mental health institutions. The admission and release of patients at mental health institutions was a problem due to lack of sufficient financial resources to provide adequate psychiatric evaluations.

National/Racial/Ethnic Minorities

There were reports of significant societal discrimination against members of the Romani and Balkan-Egyptian communities. Roma and Balkan-Egyptians faced discrimination in access to housing, employment, health care, and education. Some schools resisted accepting Romani and Balkan-Egyptian students, particularly if they appeared to be poor. Local NGOs reported that many schools that accepted Romani students marginalized them in the classroom, sometimes by physically setting them apart from other students.

In August a private property developer in Tirana forcibly evicted 37 Romani families from a building they had occupied for 10 years. The families moved to the street in front of the building. The Tirana mayor's office was unresponsive to calls to assist them with housing. The national government identified a suitable shelter for the families at a renovated former military base, and the families relocated there.

The law provides official minority status for national groups and separately for ethnolinguistic groups. The government defined Greeks, Macedonians, and

Montenegrins as national groups; Greeks constituted the largest of these. The law defined Aromanians (Vlachs) and Roma as ethnolinguistic minority groups.

The ethnic Greek minority complained about the government's unwillingness to recognize ethnic Greek towns outside communist-era "minority zones," to utilize Greek in official documents and on public signs in ethnic Greek areas, and to include a higher number of ethnic Greeks in public administration.

Societal Abuses, Discrimination, and Acts of Violence Based on Sexual Orientation and Gender Identity

The law prohibits discrimination against lesbian, gay, bisexual, and transgender (LGBT) individuals. The government's antidiscrimination commissioner registered several complaints from LGBT individuals and organizations. The commissioner issued sanctions against two senior politicians; however, the politicians ignored the sanctions. Enforcement of the law was generally weak.

In May the assembly passed an amendment that added sexual orientation and gender identity to the list of classes protected by the country's hate crime law. In April then prime minister Sali Berisha met publicly with LGBT activists and reiterated his support for their human rights and inclusion in society. In May then opposition leader and current Prime Minister Edi Rama also publicly met with LGBT activists in a highly publicized event at which he voiced his support for the community.

Despite the law and the government's formal support for LGBT rights, homophobic attitudes remained. On April 11, the media published an alleged private text message from former justice minister Eduard Halimi to Democratic Party parliamentarian Fatos Hoxha during the ombudsman's appearance at a parliamentary meeting, warning Hoxha to "not mess with the ombudsman because he supports faggots."

On May 17, activists participated in a Ride Against Homophobia, a short bicycle ride on Tirana's main boulevard. A group of men attacked the riders at a gathering after the event, throwing tear gas into a cafe where the riders had met and yelling slurs and insults. Police refused to characterize the act as a hate crime because they said no participants were physically injured.

Other Societal Violence or Discrimination

The law prohibits discrimination against persons with HIV/AIDS. There is a general social stigma against persons with HIV/AIDS, although there were no reports of violence against such individuals during the year.

Section 7. Worker Rights

a. Freedom of Association and the Right to Collective Bargaining

The law and related regulations and statutes provide the right for most workers to form independent unions, conduct legal strikes, and bargain collectively. The government effectively enforced these laws. The law prohibits members of the military and senior government officials from joining unions and requires that a trade union have at least 20 members to be registered. The law provides the right to strike for all workers except uniformed military, police, indispensable medical and hospital personnel, persons providing air traffic control and prison services, and both essential and nonessential workers in water and electrical utilities. Workers not excluded by their position exercised their right to strike.

The law prohibits anti-union discrimination and provides for the reinstatement of workers fired for union activity. These laws rarely protected domestic and migrant workers.

Civilian workers in all fields have the constitutional right to organize and bargain collectively, and the law establishes procedures for the protection of workers' rights through collective bargaining agreements. Unions representing public sector employees negotiated directly with the government. Effective collective bargaining remained difficult, and agreements were hard to enforce. Unions are often associated with political parties, and strikes sometimes became politicized. The law prohibits strikes that courts judge to be political in nature.

There is a labor inspectorate, but there were reports of arbitrary fines and ineffective enforcement.

b. Prohibition of Forced or Compulsory Labor

The law prohibits all forms of forced or compulsory labor; however, the government did not always effectively enforce the law. Enforcement was hampered because of a lack of coordination among ministries and sporadic implementation of standard operating procedures. In September the new government appointed a new national antitrafficking coordinator. The Office of the National Antitrafficking Coordinator depended heavily on international donor funding to support its operations.

Also see the Department of State's *Trafficking in Persons Report* at www.state.gov/j/tip/.

c. Prohibition of Child Labor and Minimum Age for Employment

The law sets the minimum age of employment at 16 and regulates the amount and type of labor that children under the age of 18 may perform. Children between 16 and 18 may work in certain specified jobs. While the law provides that the Ministry of Youth and Social Welfare is responsible for enforcing minimum age requirements through the courts, it did not adequately enforce the law. Labor inspectors investigated the formal labor sector, whereas most child labor occurred in the informal sector. Most labor inspections occurred in shoe and textile factories; some instances of child labor were found during these inspections.

In July the government's statistical agency and the International Labor Organization reported that 54,000 children were forced to work in domestic child labor. An estimated 43,000 children worked in farms and fishing, 4,400 in the services sector, and 2,200 in hotels and restaurants. Nearly 7 percent of children were child laborers.

The government improved cooperation between the labor inspectorate and municipal child rights units. It trained 120 inspectors in child labor monitoring and developed a child labor inspection strategy for 2013-20.

The law criminalizes exploitation of children for labor or forced services, but the government did not enforce the law effectively. Reports noted that a majority of child laborers worked as street or shop vendors, beggars, farmers, shepherds, drug runners, vehicle washers, textile factory workers, miners, or shoeshine boys. Some of the children begging on the street were second- or third-generation beggars. Research suggested that begging started as early as the age of four or five years old. While the criminal code prohibits the exploitation of children for begging, police generally did not enforce the law. The government did not provide resources for rehabilitation of children begging and living on the street.

Also see the Department of Labor's *Findings on the Worst Forms of Child Labor* at www.dol.gov/ilab/programs/ocft/tda.htm.

d. Acceptable Conditions of Work

The national minimum wage was 22,000 leks ($211) per month. According to the government's statistics agency, the average wage for government workers in the second quarter of the year was 51,700 leks ($496) per month. By comparison the national poverty threshold in 2012 was 6,472 leks ($62) per month. The statistics agency reported that average monthly wages in the public sector at the end of the second quarter of the year had increased 5.9 percent from the same quarter in 2012. The labor code requires equal pay for equal work.

The Ministry of Youth and Social Welfare is responsible for enforcing the minimum wage. While the law establishes a 40-hour workweek, individual or collective agreements typically set the actual workweek. The law establishes paid annual holidays, but only employers in the formal labor market had guaranteed rights to paid holidays. Many persons worked six days a week. The law requires payment of overtime and rest periods, but employers did not always observe these provisions. The law limits the maximum hours of work per week to 50 and provides for premium pay for overtime. The government had no standards for a minimum number of rest periods per week and rarely enforced laws related to maximum work hours, limits on overtime, or premium pay for overtime. These laws did not often apply to workers in the informal sector such as domestic employees and migrant workers.

The Ministry of Youth and Social Welfare is responsible for enforcing occupational health and safety standards and regulations. Enforcement was lacking overall. Workplace conditions frequently were very poor and, in some cases, dangerous. Penalties often did not deter violations, because law enforcement agencies lacked the tools to enforce collection and consequently rarely charged violators. There were no government programs to provide social protection for workers in the informal economy.

Wage and occupational safety standards violations occurred most frequently in the textile and shoe industries, construction, and mining.